As The Leader Grows

Ken Joslin

ISBN:

Paperback 978-1-64184-741-4

DEDICATION

Kristy, this book would not be possible without you. Thank you. To Holli, Sarah Beth, Caroline & Emma Kate, I am so proud to be your dad.

I've been blessed with many mentors in every area of my life and to each of you, I owe the debt of gratitude.

I wish to dedicate this book to all the leaders who choose a life of significance before success.

A SPECIAL NOTE...

In his book *As the Leader Grows,* Ken Joslin brings together the wisdom he gained over the last 25 years as both a minister and business builder. He brings a fresh perspective to entrepreneurship introducing ROM, Return On Mission, that highlights the successful impact of the business and not just its financial success. Along the way, his mission is to help leaders Build Confidence, Gain Clarity & Create Community.

Sharon Lechter

www.sharonlechter.com

Author of Think and Grow Rich for Women, Coauthor of Exit Rich, Outwitting the Devil, Three Feet From Gold, Rich Dad Poor Dad, and more.

TABLE OF CONTENTS

Section 3: Create Community

INTRODUCTION

I've spent the last 25 years building leaders and teams. I started as a pastor & church planter. Then, I became an entrepreneur and real estate professional building my own team. Now, I coach leaders through various programs. I've identified three distinct pillars throughout my career that helps people find significance and success in their personal lives and business: crush limited beliefs, create winning strategies, and champion a leadership culture. If you picture a three-legged table, each of those is a leg that helps people go from mundane to meaningful lives.

I started the coaching & consulting firm Grow Stack Drive in April 2020 to help business professionals **build confidence, gain clarity, & create community**. My team and I do that in several ways, including online group coaching, online courses, one-on-one consulting, live events & the Grow Stack Drive podcast. In this book, I share some of our most widely used concepts to help you grow as a leader.

Grow Stack Drive launched as the COVID pandemic was just beginning. Most people would consider this a disadvantage, but to us, it was the opposite. In a time when most businesses were retreating, we were advancing.

Over the years, I've had the pleasure of helping hundreds of people grow not only their leadership ability but also discover their purpose. By sharing what I learned along the way, I hope you can find your purpose, too. This isn't a book to celebrate my successes; it's the culmination of over thirty-plus years in business. I share real lessons from my successes, failures, and personal development.

I hope to deliver a well-rounded, clear, and actionable process for leadership development. By combining the greatest lessons from my life and work, along with advice and meaningful messages from some of my closest colleagues, I hope to give you the foundation you need to achieve more in your life.

At Grow Stack Drive, we view success through the lens of significance. One of my favorite Zig Ziglar quotes is: "You can get everything in life you want if you will just help enough other people get what they want." When we chase significance first, we will always be successful. Plus, we live life at a high level of fulfillment. I will explore that topic in depth in this book.

When God created me, He made a man passionate about identifying the purpose and potential in people and calling that out in them.

I want you to see bigger things for your life and understand there's more inside you than you realize.

I wholeheartedly believe that the path to unlocking a more powerful version of yourself is through mindset, strategy, and multiplication. Therefore, I use these steps as the framework for Grow Stack Drive and look forward to sharing how you can apply them.

In each chapter of this book, I will walk you through expelling old ways of thinking and making changes in your life. In addition, there are special affirmations and action steps at the end of each chapter to help you.

If you feel a calling to lead others, then master these skills and, by the time you finish this book, my prayer is that you see yourself just as God sees you.

Ken Joslin

SECTION 1

BUILD CONFIDENCE

In the first section, I will lay the foundation for getting your mind right and having the mental breakthroughs you need to put momentum into developing the leader within you.

1

MINDSET—THE GIFT OF EVERY DAY

How you wake up and approach every single day you have on this earth is critical to your success. I don't mean eating healthy, giving to charity, or journaling. Although those are great tools, I'm talking about how you view your life. When you wake up dreading your day and feeling like you have to instead of ***getting to***, you automatically set yourself up for failure. Instead, find joy in what you GET to do every day.

Stick around me long enough, and you'll hear me say, "If you need an alarm clock to get out of bed, your goals are not big enough."

This section is all about aligning what you want with what you have going on between your ears. Believe it or not, they aren't always congruent. I know firsthand. In 2019, I started the year with very little vision and almost no purpose. That doesn't mean on the outside I wasn't a successful realtor. My average monthly income was around $10,000 a month. The only problem was it bored me to death. I was literally working about 15 hours a week.

Before we dive in further, do you realize that waking up every day is something extraordinary? The simple act of waking up in the morning is worth more than millions of dollars. How can that be?

My friend Brad Lea illustrated this best. When I interviewed him for my podcast, he posed a question that changed my perspective and many other folks. He asked, "Would you want a million dollars in cash with no strings attached?" Well, sure, who wouldn't?!

He told my audience to think about how it'd feel to receive that million dollars. Can you picture that in your bank account right now? You'd be overjoyed, right?! But then he added a follow-up question, "Would you want that million dollars *if* you couldn't wake up tomorrow?"

That's a resounding **no way**! I really want you to ponder that for a moment. Brad's point is that we'd all be very enthusiastic if we had the cash, but waking up is worth ***more*** than the money. So why don't we wake up every day with boundless energy and enthusiasm if the gift of waking up is worth more to us than a million dollars in cash?

How might your life change if you viewed the act of just waking up as more valuable than a million bucks? Friends, start waking up with this mindset every day, and your life will change. Put a note beside your coffee pot or on a mirror—whatever you must do!—and keep this thought with you as you begin each day. If you evaluate life in those terms, you'll find it creates optimism. The things you and I think of problems become opportunities. So, give this mindset shift a try. Work to be grateful to where you view the act of waking up as more valuable than a deposit in your bank account.

Your mind is the most powerful thing on this earth. What you do with it will make or break you.

It all starts with what is going on in between your ears. To quote my good friend, Richie Dolan, "Keep in mind, when the mind does not see the proof, it confirms the obvious, that you have put yourself at risk. When you see the proof in positivity, it makes it clear that you can keep moving forward."

The most transformational change to start your morning with the right mindset is to begin the night before. Every night, I spend around 10-15 minutes planning out the next day in my Grow Stack Drive planner. This way, when I wake up, I am not reactive to what is happening but intentionally creating my day around my goals.

Mindset is one of the most essential and powerful tools you have at your disposal in both your personal and professional lives. The mindset you have can make or break you.

One of the most critical aspects of business success, and honestly, in life, is understanding what mindset is and the power behind the mindset you have. Mindset is the established set of attitudes held by someone. It is a settled way of thinking or feeling about someone or something.

When you have a growth-focused, positive mindset, you can accomplish more than you can imagine. Whatever your dreams are now as an individual or for your business are within reach with the right mindset.

The opposite is a fixed or negative mindset; it is much harder to achieve anything valuable with this mindset. Having a negative mindset will not only make it harder for you to reach your goals, but can also mean that you accomplish nothing. As you read the following chapers, ask yourself: is my mindset helping or hindering my success and ability to grow?

Are you allowing yourself to be consumed by the negative and the limiting? Or are you creating the right mindset for yourself: thinking positively, taking positive action, and creating powerful connections?

One of the most critical aspects of your development as a leader at home, church, or in business is to get your mindset right and ensure that you are okay with being who you are, regardless of who you are around and what the situation is.

"The number one reason that people are not comfortable being themselves is because they were not assured, confirmed, or protected when they were little."—Tim Storey

Throughout this book, I'll be asking you to review some parts of your past that aren't always remembered fondly. I will also walk you through some of the most common limiting beliefs my clients and I have faced. It's not always easy to confront these but, as you go through this more profound work on yourself, know that it is 100% *okay* to be who you are, as you are.

I want to leave you with a powerful quote from my good friend Tim Storey, "If you are looking to help others by assuring, confirming, and protecting those around you, you must first be comfortable with yourself. And realize, you are a work in progress. You are going through recovery and discovery. If you wait until you are completely recovered before mentoring someone else, it will be a long time. Singularly, you are in recovery and discovery at the same time. You have to know that grace will fill in the gaps. You have to know and believe that God's grace is so within you that you have the strength to reach out to others who are probably hurting worse."

TAKE ACTION NOW:

As you go through the next few hours and days, examine your mindset. What is your mindset like right now: are you focused on changing and growing, or focused on believing things "are just this way" and won't change for the better? In what ways can you adjust your mindset as you walk through your days?

2
RETURN ON MISSION

I'm sure you've heard the term ROI, or return on investment. It's typically a performance measure to evaluate a project or business deal. For example, when people invest in stocks and the value rises, they have a good ROI. Now that we're clear on ROI, I want you to forget all about it!

I've found that across the board, there are many transactional relationships. Many of those people lack character and integrity. I'm not saying it is intentional, but viewing interactions as transactional is definitely a powerful idea that permeates modern society. I see it all the time, and I always tell my clients that they only have two options when approaching others.

Option one, you can see everyone through the lens of creating a potential relationship that might add value to your life. Option two, you can see everyone as dollar signs and transactions. More often than not, transactional people end up losing everything they build. On the other hand, if you can make it about relationships, you'll make more money than you ever thought possible.

Instead of ROI, I use the term ROM, for return on **mission,** when I speak to my colleagues and clients. Return on mission is very similar to significance versus success, which I cover later in this book. A return on investment means you're driven by revenue. Something far more powerful than money drives return on mission—your WHY drives it.

I believe that all of us are looking for fulfillment that goes beyond investments.

While other coaches say things like "Scale to sale," I believe most of my clients want to build a business they ***don't*** want to sell. They want to leave an impact.

I hear this most often at our Grow Stack Drive bootcamps. I bring game-changing thought leaders to these three-day workshops that I host throughout the year. At the end of the bootcamp, the attendees most often comment that they leave feeling they can grow their **dreams**, not just a business. They also report having more focus and an action plan to make that a reality.

The feedback from one attendee sticks out in my mind. I'd just wrapped a weekend bootcamp and had asked for volunteers to give me feedback on the value of the bootcamp. Justin came on camera and answered questions, just like the other volunteers. But when asked how bootcamp helped him get results in his business, he said he'd already seen gains both in revenue and spiritually.

Of course, that intrigued me, the cameraman, and anyone in earshot and we wanted to hear more. Justin explained he'd experienced an "aha" moment of clarity during that trip and unlocked his genuine passion for wanting to motivate and inspire kids. Turns out that his heart was in creating opportunities for kids in juvenile homes and foster care. He had stunning and heartbreaking statistics about these kids, and it moved him to do more than he'd ever thought possible. Before he walked away, he said, "I now realize how valuable I am and what I can do."

By the time he left, he'd lined up meetings with a social media guru, his local Chamber of Commerce, and three additional meetings to discuss partnerships that would make his dream a reality. There really aren't words to describe how I feel every time I think about Justin's story. There isn't a measurement system for that type of growth, which is why I always encourage you to have a return on mission mindset.

TAKE ACTION NOW:

Grab some blank paper and start writing about what really sets your soul on fire. What are you most passionate about? What is your mission on this earth? If money wasn't in the equation, what would you do to leave an impact on this world? There are no right answers. I just want you to take a little time alone and be honest to discover your own return on mission mindset.

3

DAILY AFFIRMATIONS TO GROW

In order to change your life, you must start with what is right between your ears. We are going to be working through some uncomfortable, some deep, and some incredibly important aspects of mindset in this book. My aim is to help you align where you are now with where you want to be and bridge the gap between the two. In my Grow Stack Drive Code Courses, I dig deeper into strategies that make this possible, but for now, just focus on getting your mindset right.

The quickest way to adjust your mindset is to practice daily affirmations.

I will provide you with seven affirmations to repeat every single day. I ask that you come up with five more affirmations that are meaningful to you.

Don't sweep the importance of this under the rug. At least twice a day, every day, I repeat my affirmations. I always speak them once in the morning, before I do anything else, and once at night, right before I go to bed. I ask this of my entire community as well.

My four personal affirmations are:

I will live a life where my heart, head, and relationships are in alignment.
I am loved by those closest to me.
I am worthy in the eyes of my Savior.
I am enough because I am His child.

The whole concept behind the first affirmation is to bridge any gap in these areas. My heart is where I dream. It's where I paint the picture. It's where my vision and passion are born, and that's what fuels me every day. My mind or my head is where my mindset is located. It's where my belief system is located. It is my belief system that determines my actions. My heart does not determine my actions.

What I think is what I speak, what I speak is what I do, and what I do determines my legacy. So, if my heart and my head are not in alignment, I'm going to dream, but I will not see those dreams come to pass. My mindset and my belief system aren't in alignment. All of that goes into crushing limiting beliefs, and I dive into those deep in the next chapter.

If my head and my heart are not in alignment, the hope that I have in my heart will erode. I recently drilled down my personal affirmations to include my relationships being in alignment as well. And those things all have to be in order. Number one, my heart has to see a big vision, which is why the Grow Stack Drive family writes our goals down twice a day. It's why we practice gratitude and affirmations and why we list the top three things we need to work on each day.

Once my heart fires up and starts dreaming, I work on my mindset. Our business is like a multiple-story building, and on every story, we hit a new ceiling. Often, that ceiling—that point that stops us from leveling up—is a mindset. Perhaps I deal with lots of fear and insecurity early on in my life or business.

As my business grows, I will have to deal with fresh fear and insecurity on a different level. It doesn't mean when I deal with it once it's gone. It's no different from your spiritual walk with Christ. You may have heard someone say, "New levels, new devils." It's a cheesy preacher joke, but it's true. Growth in life and business will require me to be prepared for the changes and challenges ahead, so I aim to live a life where my heart, head, and relationships align.

When I have those first two things aligned, things happen. Incredible things. My relationships get in alignment. I'm watching this happen for me now, as a new season brings fresh relationships into my life. Now I'm surrounded with relationships I can add value to and relationships which help us get meaningful results toward my mission of helping business professionals build confidence, get clarity, and create community.

My affirmation, "I am enough because I am His child," is new as well. Previously I used, "I am enough. I am worthy. And I am loved." As you can see, my affirmations are fluid and always evolving. I use these affirmations every time I hit a challenging moment or things get hard. I turn to my affirmations and say these whenever I'm struggling throughout the day. It might be once a day, or it might be ten times a day; it just depends on what the day looks like.

I encourage you to write some of your own affirmations down and say them out loud every day. As you create your own affirmations, dig in and get clear, powerful statements on the ***why*** behind them. To help you get started, here are a few we use in our online courses:

1. I will fail and embrace failure as long as I have learned something.
2. I am afraid of NOT doing it.
3. I want something for you, not *from* you.

4. I have the ability and the power to create all the abundance and prosperity I desire.
5. My thoughts do not control me—I control my thoughts and today, my thoughts will be free, happy, and positive.
6. My mind is open to possibilities and free of resistance.
7. I am grateful for every person who contributes to my happiness, experiences, and life.

Before we wrap up, let's quickly discuss each affirmation and why it's crucial to a leader's mindset.

I will fail and embrace failure as long as I have learned something.

Failure comes for all of us. Our job & responsibility is to learn from that failure.

I am afraid of NOT doing it.

I can't sit still. I ***must*** act on the passion and desire I have in my heart.

I want something for you, not from you.

Imagine relationships you have in your life when your goal is to help other people. Remember, what Zig Ziglar said: "You can get everything in life you want if you will just help enough other people get what they want."

I have the ability and the power to create all the abundance and prosperity I desire.

No one is in charge of your future other than you.

My thoughts do not control me—I control my thoughts and today, my thoughts will be free, happy, and positive.

I am in control of my thoughts and my mindset. I have the power to change my reality.

My mind is open to possibilities and free of resistance.

Fight to get outside of the box and believe in bigger things.

I am grateful for every person who contributes to my happiness, experiences, and life.

I always say that one characteristic of a passionate leader is that they're intentional and adding value. And for that last affirmation, a great way to practice is to pick your phone up. You can pause and do it right now. Text two or three people who have made a difference in your life, and simply tell them, "Thank you."

Saying these daily affirmations out loud every morning and every night will help transform your life. Next, I want to uncover the reasons you stop yourself from taking action and replace that with new ways of thinking.

TAKE ACTION NOW:

Write out five affirmations. These do not have to be perfect or permanent; you can revise them as needed.

4

IDENTIFY, REMOVE, AND REPLACE LIMITED BELIEF SYSTEMS

One of the biggest deterrents to achieving what you set out to do is the belief system you hold. Having a limited belief system curtails what you believe is possible for you and what you will allow in your life. These belief systems restrict how you show up for your life. They keep you from seeing what is truly achievable for you.

We develop belief systems over time and through experience. Limited belief systems form in several ways. They include experiences you might have had as a child or even as an adult, the uncertainty you might have about your abilities, and even the environment you are in and who you surround yourself with.

Common Limited Belief Systems

Limiting beliefs do just that—they limit you. They limit your potential and your ability to achieve what you want. We will tackle limited belief systems that I have found to be the biggest barriers to both my success and the success of those around me. The limited belief systems we will dig into are fear, scarcity, shame, insecurity, comparison, and success. This chapter, will detail how leaders commonly struggle with those and how to unlock yourself from their grip.

Before we dive in, I want to share a transformational moment where I identified a limited belief. I spent several years as a church planter struggling financially, personally, and in our church. Even though finances aren't the single most important thing in planting a church, they are very important. I was at the 10x Bootcamp, and I had a breakthrough moment listening to the amazing speakers. What I'd thought possible in my life was small peanuts. I told my friend and mentor Grant Cardone, "I am here to blow the lid off my mindset of what is a lot of money." Once you identify your own limited belief systems, you're ready to remove and replace them.

As I go through the discussion of common limited belief systems I have encountered and seen within my organizations and in my coaching, I will give you tools and affirmations to use so that you can remove and replace them.

Something to keep a lookout for as you challenge your limited belief systems is if you are faking it until you make it. Are you showing up unauthentically trying to prove you are above this limited belief and in a better place than you actually are, financially or otherwise?

Working through limited belief systems will push you and require authenticity in yourself and your processes beyond what you may have experienced before.

Lean into this and allow it to guide you. When you live in your authenticity, you attract more people—more people who like who you actually are, not who you *appear* to be. Being real will help you address the limited belief systems you are attached to.

Breaking Down Limited Belief Systems

In the next few pages, you will learn how to define and redefine each of the key limited belief systems. We will work through some examples and reframe how each of these exists in your life. Each of these lessons aims to help you step away from your limited belief system and identify your truth. You may want to grab some paper or a notebook as we go through these exercises.

FEAR

I define fear as an unpleasant emotion caused by the belief that someone or something is dangerous and likely to cause pain or be a threat. Fear is one of the biggest limited belief systems that people struggle with, and it shows up in several ways.

Because of fear, people cannot move forward or achieve greatness. It has the incredible power to hold people back from achieving their truest potential. If you are afraid to make the first move, it's time to step out of your comfort zone. I guarantee you will not achieve what you set out to achieve, and you will not have the significance or success you desire until you learn to master fear.

At some point, every single person experiences fear. It is a natural part of life to worry, to experience discomfort, and to fear something. The difference between having a limited belief system of fear and merely experiencing fear is ***what you do*** when faced with it. Do you take action despite being afraid or run away?

"God knows your frame, your structure, your makeup… and calls you to do sturdy projects. God calls shaky people to do sturdy projects because he knows he is bigger than our shakiness." - Tim Storey

When overcoming the limited belief system of fear, it is important to first identify the fears you have experienced. When you look back, what would you say is or has been your biggest fear?

Defining the Limited Belief System of Fear

To give you a more refined definition, fear is the belief that if I step out of my comfort zone, bad things will happen. Something will go terribly wrong when I put myself out there. I fail; therefore, I am a failure.

We are born with two fears: the fear of falling and the fear of loud noises. We learn all other fears. So, if we once learned them, we can unlearn them. This limited belief system has kept countless people from achieving their own greatness, moving into success, and living a life filled with joy and happiness.

Replace Fear with Courage

The truth about fear is that it takes courage to overcome it. You must willingly step out of your comfort zone. This is arduous work, but it is important. Fear can be used as fuel. Fuel to step out of your comfort zone. Fuel to achieve what might be a little frightening right now. Fuel to step into the greatest version of yourself.

Are you ready to change from fear to courage?

AFFIRMATION:

I will fail and embrace failure as long as I have learned something.

Remember what John Maxwell said in his book, *Failing Forward*, "If you're not failing, you're probably not really moving forward."

Recite the affirmation we discussed previously: "I am afraid of NOT doing it." We've got to get to a place where we are uncomfortable staying put. We see our vision down the road. When you feel fear creeping in, tell yourself, "the fear will not hold me back and let me stay where I am right now. I have to move forward."

TAKE ACTION NOW:

List out some fears you have on one side of a sheet of paper, then list out at least one way you can be courageous in the face of each of those fears on the other side.

SCARCITY

Scarcity creates the illusion that there is not enough to go around. It preys on insufficiency or shortness of supply. As a limited belief, it can cause exceptional people to fall short of getting what they desire.

A perfect and most recent example of scarcity was during the COVID-19 pandemic. Our economy had over 1.5 trillion *extra* dollars introduced in fewer than six months.

Scarcity is devoted to the idea of lack. This lack can include a lack of resources, lack of money, or lack of anything else. When you have a limited belief system of scarcity, you truly believe there is not enough of whatever you need or desire to go around.

Often, this mindset drives successful people to hoard information or simply stop sharing it. Those with a scarcity limited belief system are not willing to promote the work of others, collaborate, or congratulate others when they succeed. One way we combat this at Grow Stack Drive is to promote other speakers, authors, and coaches in our community.

In what ways have you experienced scarcity? I grew up in a single-parent home from the age of eight, and scarcity was all around us. So just going to McDonald's was a real treat for me. I remember the first pair of Nike's my Mom bought for me. They cost $55, and I was in the seventh grade. I'll never forget it. I exclaimed, "Oh my God, I have NIKES!"

Defining the Limited Belief System of Scarcity

As we have previously discussed, scarcity is the belief system that there is not enough to go around. When people are experiencing a scarcity mindset, they will hoard things, information, or resources as opposed to sharing and helping others grow.

The quote from Zig Ziglar previously mentioned—when you help enough people get what they want, you will eventually get what you want—is absolutely true. The scarcity mindset thinks, "if I don't keep this close, or if I share, there won't be enough for me. I can't be successful if I give or share too much."

Replace Scarcity with Abundance

There really is enough for everyone. In fact, there is more than enough for everyone. To combat scarcity, I want you to work toward reframing your thoughts from scarcity to abundance. When you live in abundance, there is always more than enough. There is always plenty. You can give more than you take and receive a tremendous amount of fortune and growth.

A scarcity mindset blocks you from blessing other people.

Recently, I was at a Waffle House, grabbing some dinner after a basketball game with my guys. I walked in around 11:30 p.m., and I was the only person in the diner. I sat down, ate dinner, and as I was finishing up, a guy walked in with three young boys. As

I watched, it became apparent my server was their mother. I walked up and was paying my bill, chatting, and I just asked her a question. I said, "Hey, was that your husband dropping off your three children?" And she just had a look of sadness come over her. She said, "No, sir. My husband died last month and left these three kids and me."

Immediately, I felt stirred and led by God to give her what I could. I pulled out my wallet again and counted the cash inside. I had about $240 in twenty-dollar bills. I knew from having my own kids at home that school would start in a week. I pulled the money out and said to her, "Listen, this is for you. I want you to know God told me He loves you and He hasn't forgotten about you."

This newly widowed woman began to cry, walked around the front of the counter at Waffle House, and I spent a couple of minutes praying for her and for her three boys. Because I have overcome the limited belief of scarcity, I knew I could give that woman all my cash, and more would come to me.

AFFIRMATION:

I want something **for** you, not from you.

When you get around people who want something for you and not from you, it's refreshing. I ask this question a lot: when you walk into a room, do people gravitate toward you or away from you? Listen, when you live in abundance and live in the mindset and affirmation, "I want something for people, and not from them," people will naturally want to be around you.

TAKE ACTION NOW:

One side of a sheet of paper list out how you have lived with scarcity. Then list out at least one way you can live in more abundance on the opposite side.

SHAME

The limited belief system of shame is one of the most deep-rooted and intimate limited belief systems. It can run deep into who you are as a person and is completely worth the work it takes to overcome and work through it.

Shame is a powerful feeling of humiliation or distress caused by the consciousness of wrong or foolish behavior. Someone other than yourself causes this feeling a majority of the time.

Shame can emerge from many things, including your upbringing and unresolved mistakes you made, among several others. The shame limited belief system takes time to not only identify but also resolve.

When addressing shame, you must consider taking a step or two back and really digging into the root cause of the shame you are experiencing. I encourage you to take the time you need to get below the surface level of what shame you hold on to. When processing shame, first consider what it really means to you. Who do you feel is holding you accountable for the mistakes you have made?

"For a lot of us who were raised in church feel like we are going to get treated as our sins deserve, but the Bible says for as high as the heavens are above the earth so great is his love for those who honor him… for God knows your frame, your makeup, your structure." —Tim Storey

What shame are you holding on to?

Defining the Limited Belief System of Shame

Experiencing shame often creates a deep-rooted belief that your past mistakes define who you are now and have a profound effect on your ability to either succeed or fail. Shame draws from the idea that because you have failed, you are wrong. Shame can show up in several ways, but overall will prevent you from achieving more.

When people enroll in our Grow course, they get an exclusive viewing of a conversation between me and my good friend Nate May. Nate has helped shape the message, the voice, and the brand of some of the most well-known speakers and influencers across multiple industries. In addition, he's had to dive deep and study the limited belief system of shame as part of his own journey.

People frequently confuse guilt and shame. Guilt is all about feeling wrong about something you *do*. Shame is the feeling that *you're just wrong*; like there's something wrong with *you*. Nate explained the difference between guilt and shame so well that I felt it was worth sharing with you.

Nate said, "Guilt says, 'I feel bad that I did something wrong.' Shame says that 'there is something wrong with me.' And so there's a big difference between those two differentiators. You literally think (because of shame) that there's something inherently wrong with you."

Replace Shame with Unashamed

The truth about shame is that you are ***not*** the mistakes you have made. In fact, you are *far from* the mistakes you have made. Instead of leading with shame, try reframing your internal dialogue to learn from the mistakes. There are great lessons in the actions we have taken, in the failures experienced, and in the times we were at our worst or most vulnerable.

Mistakes don't prove that we are bad.
They just prove that we are human.

As long as you own it and make it right, shame can't control you. When I was talking with Nate, we discussed deep ownership. Nate says, "When you're changing a belief system, there's a natural process of going through pain and shame. Parts of you are wrestling with what's going on, but deep ownership is the first step. So, people don't typically deeply own it because when you deeply own something that you've done, it's painful."

AFFIRMATION:

I will not stop moving forward because I have failed in the past.

TAKE ACTION NOW:

Grab a piece of paper or open a blank spreadsheet. List out some mistakes and things you have done that bring you shame on the left-hand side. Then share the truths about each of these on the right.

INSECURITY

Insecurity is a lack of confidence or assurance. I often see insecurity presented as self-doubt. I also find this to be a common struggle when I speak to my community and go one-on-one with leaders. Insecurity keeps people within the confines of their comfort zone or, worse, keeps them behind the scenes, never coming forward.

There are so many insecurities that people struggle with. Each insecurity can and **will** hold folks back. The insecurities you have or have experienced in the past may have started from a very young age, so similar to addressing the limited belief system of shame, you will need to take a couple of steps back and really get to the core of where your insecurities come from.

What insecurities are you experiencing right now?

What have you experienced in the past?

Defining the Limited Belief System of Insecurity

As you may have learned or probably realized in some capacity before, insecurity is the perceived notion that you are not qualified to do what you are doing. Most people are insecure about areas in which they may lack skills, abilities, or connections. They believe these are necessary to advance their life beyond what they have now.

Replace Insecurity with Security

We have defined what insecurity is, and the impact that this limited belief system has. Insecurity is deep-rooted in your mindset. Your insecurities are simply false statements that you believe to be true. **It is okay** to feel worried, scared, or unsure, but you must work through what is *really* stopping you from going after what you want. Insecurity is the barrier to your personal success.

AFFIRMATION:

I will be strong in my decisions even if I make mistakes. If this guy or gal can do it, so can I. When I encourage you, it fills me with encouragement as well. Encouraging others is a giant eraser for my own insecurities.

TAKE ACTION NOW:

List out some insecurities you have on one side of a sheet of paper, then list out all the things you are secure with on the other side. What actions can you take to replace your insecurities with security?

COMPARISON

"Comparison is the thief of joy" is a common statement and entirely true. When you live with the limited belief system of comparison, you are hyper-focused on how you and your work stack up against everyone else. Comparison makes you believe that nothing you do is ever good enough. Adversely, nothing that anyone else does is good enough.

Comparison creates two false beliefs. First, it makes you feel as if you don't measure up to someone ahead of you. Second, it gives you a false sense of being further ahead or better than someone else. Both false beliefs create an unhealthy mindset and hinder your ability to achieve more.

Comparison controls how you view and react to experiences. Comparing yourself to others holds you back from achieving more and staying aligned with who you really are. For most anyone absorbing this material, we spend too much time in the comparison trap. Likewise, when we think about God, we spend precious little time thinking about what ***He*** thinks about us and what we should think about ourselves.

Who are you comparing yourself to?

What comparisons have you been struggling with?

Defining the Limited Belief System of Comparison

The basis of comparison is stacking yourself against those around you and putting your successes or failures under a microscope, alongside the successes and failures of others. It entails positioning your wins and losses against those who are at a higher achievement level or playing a totally different game than you. Comparison is robbing you of your own happiness.

Replace Comparison with Confidence

Comparison is unnecessary. As we addressed with scarcity, there is more than enough of whatever you desire or whatever you are working toward to go around. It is okay to have compassion, to share other people's accomplishments, and to cheer on other people doing what you're doing.

AFFIRMATION:

I am not comparing myself to the person next to me; I am comparing me just to myself. I am more interested in collaboration than competition. I have compassion for everyone who is out there looking to achieve more.

ACTION:

List out people or things you compare yourself or success to on one side of a sheet of paper., On the other side, list out at least one way you can be confident to combat each comparison.

SUCCESS

What does success currently mean to you? I think we view success as a positive thing in most regards, and it can be. Success is all about achieving goals, growing monetarily, and accomplishing what you set out to do. But I want you to understand that it is a limited belief system. As I will approach it and have experienced it, success is a self-focused, selfish action of accumulating more. It focuses entirely on the accumulation of personal gains.

Success in this regard is not about others; it is all about what you get and how you are accumulating wealth. Thus, success focuses primarily on "what's in it for me" and not "what I can do to serve and help others."

When you have a limited belief in success, you cannot give as much as you are attempting to receive. What this actually does is hinder your ability to receive as much as you truly desire or can.

Can you identify at least three limited beliefs you have around success?

Defining the Limited Belief System of Success

As we have uncovered, success is the perceived idea of wealth, accumulation of things, and achievement. Success is a self-focused, selfish ideal of what it means to have. When you focus on success, you miss out on so much more.

Replace Success with Significance

Striving for significance will always bring success. Success doesn't always guarantee significance. I get deeper into the difference between significance and success later in the book.

AFFIRMATION:

I know and believe that it is more important to be significant than it is to be successful.

TAKE ACTION NOW:

List out some successes you have had or desire on one side of a sheet of paper. Now list ways you can live a life of more significance on the other side.

Reflections on Limited Beliefs

Now that we have broken down the misconceptions of these limited belief systems and got more aligned with the hidden truths behind them, it's time to replace those old thoughts with new truths. We have additional tools available for hashing through limited belief systems. Visit GrowStackDrive.com to learn more.

5

INCREMENTAL, NOT MONUMENTAL

When determining where your focus is and should go, think incrementally, not monumentally. Small, daily disciplined decisions over time ALWAYS equal monumental results. Success CANNOT escape you if you do the right things every day. Don't just assume that because you have this grand vision it will happen overnight.

There is no such thing as an overnight success. It took me 20 years to become the "overnight success" you may see me as now. I have been adding value to clients' lives for the past 20 years. If we focus on incremental for long enough and on every block of time, eventually, incremental change will turn into monumental change.

Don't get me wrong, I have big goals for my life. I want to grow the number of agents in my real estate company this year. I want to do millions in real estate transactions. I want to bring in more one-on-one clients and in-person events. In every area of my life, I have ambitious goals. I'll talk more about those later, but the point I want to make is that it starts with small steps every single day to reach those giant goals.

A good example to share with you is my morning routine. It never changes. In the past year, I maybe had four or five days where I didn't stick to this *exact* routine. The same is true for my bedtime routine.

It's not enough just to write goals every single day. You've got to get to work on those goals. You've got to move forward, and that's what I did on a bitter December day after I walked out of a meeting with Grant Cardone. I called Nate May, and I flew back to Atlanta. There, we spent almost five hours at a coffee shop really planning out the future.

We did not know what Grow Stack Drive was. We didn't have the Grow Stack Drive Code or the online courses outlined. Those concepts didn't even exist because we did not know what that our finished products looked like, but we knew we had passion and desire. Not just a passion and desire, but we had an **obligation** to get into action and help people.

Taking action has changed me on the inside in addition to my business career. It's done the same for those in my network. I've seen clients like Melissa Stewart, Dylan Pollard, Cynthia Caughie, and James

Rich whose businesses have all grown exponentially over the past year. It's because they get the concept of incremental growth.

I was at a retreat with some top performers and my friend, an accountant, author, and businesswoman Sharon Lechter said something to the group that has stuck with me. She said, "You need motion, not magic." She was absolutely correct.

People often ask me and my coaching clients how we do it and the answer is usually the same: we show up every day to make incremental changes, not monumental ones. Motion, not magic.

For those who follow me on social media, especially on Instagram, you know that one area of my life that I have tackled is my health. I was at a Division I Umpire Camp when a clinician told me, "Ken, you've got a great feel for the game and you have a great rapport with the players & coaches, but you have got to lose some weight." I knew I wasn't in the best shape of my life, but that really was an eye-opening moment when I heard it from someone else.

I've lost over 60 pounds in the last 18 months as I write this chapter. How? Because every single day I take incremental steps by showing up at the gym and watching what I eat. Those changes took a long time to show. If I'd given up or stopped along the way, I wouldn't have reaped the results. I didn't drop the weight all at once. Sometimes I would weigh in and have only lost one or two pounds from the previous time I weighed myself!

I know someone reading this feels stuck in an area of their life. You're stuck and you may even think, *I can't seem to get out of my own way, Ken*! Here's what I want you to remember, first downs, not touchdowns. A first down is moving the ball ten yards. Don't think about an 80-yard ball. Don't think about trying to throw 40 yards. Just start getting those first downs and guess what will happen? You build momentum. With continued smaller successes, bigger wins will come.

TAKE ACTION NOW:

List out areas of your life where you feel stuck. What are ten small tasks you can take to get closer to what you want in these areas?

SECTION 2

GAIN CLARITY

The "Stack" in Grow Stack Drive is all about getting to the core of what it takes to build a sound and actionable strategy. Stack is naturally the next step because without a great mindset, nothing is achievable and without the right strategy, things will always remain as they are. We stack the right strategy to the right mindset during this portion of the journey.

6
THE POWER OF A WINNING STRATEGY

I am looking forward to getting deep with you on some of the most important processes you could ever incorporate into your life. When you have the right strategies in place, the world completely opens up. You can achieve so much more by being aligned in your mindset and having the strategy to support your dreams.

I created this section to help individuals and business executives create the right strategies to propel their personal and professional goals forward. Following the Grow Stack Drive Code aligns the four key areas that every leader and individual needs to master: culture, goals, time, and inner circle.

Every morning I wake up to
blank pages then I write my story.
The question is, what are you writing?

Throughout this section, I will challenge you to think critically and put plans into place which may be outside of your comfort zone. I am honored to lead you through one of the most powerful tools I have ever used. As an accomplished business coach and real estate expert, I have spent the better half of my life inadvertently creating this material, and wholeheartedly living every lesson.

I want you to create effective strategies to achieve more in your personal and professional life. We are will work through powerful strategies that you can apply to any aspect of your life. If you want more detailed resources, consider visiting GrowStackDrive.com/book to help as you go through this chapter.

To create a winning strategy, you must follow a sound and replicable process. We'll first break down the steps to creating and implementing a winning strategy. You can replicate and incorporate these steps into any development strategy you create for yourself or your business.

The steps to creating a powerful, winning strategy are: define your core values, create your goals, raise the bar, create your filters, and win every single day.

TAKE ACTION NOW:

Write out the following affirmations and repeat them daily as you work through this section of the book.

1. My core values guide my day, and every decision I make is in alignment with these values.
2. I am 100% committed to making my goals a reality.
3. I let go of all pessimism and doubt that I will achieve my goals.
4. I further my career with every action I take.
5. I write down the action steps needed to reach my goals.
6. Every positive action I take accelerates my progress.
7. I am grateful for each and every person who contributes to my happiness, experiences, and life.

7

DEFINE CORE VALUES

Without core values, it is unclear to both you and others what it is that you stand for. Core values are the backbone of each strategy you have because they are the backbone of who you are. Each person should have their own set of core values, which translate into their business and entire life.

Before you build any winning strategy, you must first define your core values. Once you stand for something and have it defined, it becomes much easier to create a strategy that is in alignment with your values.

Core values have been big to me for years. When pastoring a church, core values are enormous. The first year that I attended Acquire the Fire, hosted by Ron Luce, I learned about core values, along with 600 or 700 youth pastors and leaders. Acquire the Fire was a big, Christian conference with 15,000-17,000 kids in attendance each year. During a leadership development session I first heard about core values, and this was when I defined them for myself.

That day, I wrote a mission statement: "Worship. Change. Teach the authority and truth of God's word that creates an army of young people to make a world-wide difference for the kingdom of God." I literally wrote it down 22 years ago and I can still rattle it off from memory today because it changed my life.

I also wrote three years of vision as well that day: to raise a specific amount of money, build a building of a specific size, and have a specific number of students in my youth ministry. From that point to the next year, we grew from less than 20 kids to about 170 kids a week in a room we couldn't fit them in. I couldn't even get all the kids in. They were standing outside! We raised about $75,000 and built a 7,200 square foot auditorium, one of the top of its kind in the country.

That's really when core values sunk in for me. After hearing Ron speak and following through on my vision, I realized their importance. Core values help us navigate the journey. They anchor point A to point B. You can say, "Here's where we are, here's where we're going to go." Core values are the vehicle that gives you the direction. Core values also show a team, "This is how we carry ourselves."

Pat Lencioni is a wonderful thought leader whose work I admire. In his phenomenal book, *Five Dysfunctions of a Team*, he talks a lot about core values. Pat's probably my favorite author in leadership and culture, as well as health and culture of teams. There's a podcast episode that Pat did with Ken Coleman on the EntreLeadership show. I've listened to this podcast at least 200 times. On it, he talks about healthy organizations, and Ken asks him, "What percentage of organizations do you think are healthy?" Pat answers 10 to 15%, which is just not very many. Core values are a powerful thing for organizational health.

Pat Lencioni goes on to say that most companies have core values, but they are just a plaque that hangs on the wall in the hallway. No one talks about them. That's so true! I teach the importance of core values to all my one-on-one consulting clients. In fact, I just met with one of my clients in Atlanta along with his two top guys, and together we walked through the process of creating five core values with corresponding taglines. Identifying the core values is the first challenge, but condensing them into memorable and effective taglines is extremely important as well.

I remember at the beginning of my career, one of my very first coaching clients presented me with three giant paragraphs when I asked about her core values. I told her that no one in her company could remember them all, but she disagreed. To prove the point, I pulled out my phone and called one of her top managers on speaker phone and asked what the core values of the company were. You can guess what happened next if you've ever worked at a company that just hangs something on the wall and doesn't use it. The manager hesitated a beat and then stuttered, "Um, well, I think I signed something when I first started…" Awkward!

That's all I needed to hear and we hung up. I continued working with that client and from those hefty paragraphs we detected four words that were her core values. We added a tagline for each of them and now, core values are a major part of her processes. When that client onboards somebody newly hired or when she has to let somebody go, she refers to the core values.

The fundamental beliefs you hold as an individual or your company define your core values. They are the guiding principles of what you stand for and how you expect people within your organization to act.

Typically, core values are unwavering and they should rarely change. They are steadfast no matter what the situation. Core values always represent what you stand for. They are the truest representation of who you are as the company leader. Everyone has core values. They are the code from which each person lives and works. It is important to define the three to five values that accurately represent your belief system.

What are your core values?

To identify your core values, I want you to take some time and really think about what is most meaningful for you as a person and for you as a professional. Think about what you stand for; what is important for you to represent to the world around you?

Consider:

What are the most important beliefs you have for yourself or your company?
What do you stand for?
What do you believe in?

If you already have core values defined, review them and ensure they align with where you are and what you want to achieve. Will these values going to take you from point A to point B?

AFFIRMATION:

My core values guide my day and every decision I make is in alignment with these values.

TAKE ACTION NOW:

If you don't already have them, list your core values. Try to pick between 3-5 and define *why* these are your core values.

8

CREATE GOALS

Once you have defined or aligned your core values with where you are right now, the next step is to identify your goals. Goals are an incredibly important aspect of creating a strategy because they give you an idea of where you are heading and what you are working toward. I always set goals in the three categories below, and in this order.

Personal Goals

Personal goals are always the first goals to start with. They are the ones that ultimately drive the most success. Personal goals are the goals for which you care most deeply. Personal goals can be goals you have for your entire life, where you want to go, what you want to do, or how you want to live out your days in retirement. The possibilities are endless. Consider: what do you want from your life?

Professional Goals

Once you have identified your personal goals, determine what you want from your professional life. What do the next 10, 20, 30, 40, or 50+ years of your working life look like? What do you want to achieve in your professional life? Are you focused on leaving a legacy or achieving success? Professional goals give you the basis for how you will spend a significant amount of your waking hours. How do you want to leave your mark on the professional space around you and your ecosystem?

Financial Goals

The third set of goals to establish is your financial goals. How are you going to support your personal and professional goals? What would be the ideal financial situation for you? Financial goals can bring more depth and concreteness to both your personal and professional goals. Financial goals are tangible and can tie into everything you want to achieve in your life.

When writing out your goals in the three categories above, answer the following question: what do you want to achieve? To uncover the answer, write all the things that you want to achieve with your strategy. Give yourself enough time to dig deep into what it is you want for yourself and what you want to accomplish.

AFFIRMATION:

I am 100% committed to making my goals a reality.

TAKE ACTION NOW:

Spend a minimum of ten minutes writing your six to twelve-month goals for each of the three main categories: personal, professional, and financial.

9

RAISE THE BAR

I know you invested a lot of time t come up with your goals. You gave it serious thought and were intentional in writing what you want from your personal and professional lives, as well as what you desire financially. Goal setting doesn't stop there. I want to challenge you to think BIGGER, to get a little (or a lot) more uncomfortable and stretch yourself.

Create ridiculous goals that you do not know how you are going to achieve.

BHAGs

More than 20 years ago, I learned from a good friend of mine I previously mentioned, Ron Luce, the idea behind Big Hairy Audacious Goals. Those are BHAGs (bee-hagz). That sounds silly if you've never heard of them before, but this is what they teach at Harvard

Business School. I want you to incorporate these into your life. That's right, it's time for you to create some Big Hairy Audacious Goals.

Whatever goals you wrote, I want you to make them bigger—double, triple, quadruple, or even ten times bigger! Start thinking outside of what you *know* you can achieve and beyond what is imaginable right now. If there were **no** limits, what would your goals be? What do you REALLY want? That's where you need to start with writing your BHAGs.

AFFIRMATION:

I let go of all pessimism and doubt that I will achieve my goals.

ACTION:

Review the goals you previously wrote out and make them bigger. If they feel "doable," they aren't big enough. Listen. If your goals don't make you uncomfortable, they're not the right goals. If you need an alarm clock to wake up in the morning, you don't have the right goals.

10

RUN EVERYTHING THROUGH A FILTER

My life transformed when I created a blueprint for it. That blueprint became my core values. I also call these core values my "filters" because I filter everything I do through them. I clarify all of my decisions, including what projects I take on and how I use my time, using these values as a guide.

We utilize core values starting at the very first job interview with somebody at my company. We tell them our company's core values are **passion, focus, intentionality, teachability, and flexibility**. Passion is how we attack our day. Focus is how we dominate our calendar. Intentionality means we're intentional in how we speak to one another and our clients. Teachability means we're not only open to feedback, but we actively pursue feedback. Flexibility reminds us we live in a fluid world. We better be open and willing to change.

I'll walk through all five core values and explain each of them in more depth. When I have my daily team meetings, the first thing we do is share business wins. The second thing we do is talk about the top three priorities we need to work on. The third thing we always do is talk about one core value. I pull in examples of the core value at work in our culture. We hire and promote people using our core values as a filter. They are that critical to our company.

PASSION

Passion is the fuel and drive to get you what you desire when trouble arises. It is not your personality; it is energy. Passion is just an expression of how you go after what you are trying to achieve. Passion is the fuel in your tank that keeps you going.

Passion is how you attack the day. Remember, if you need an alarm clock to get out of bed, your goals are not big enough. Consider whether or not there is something intrinsically driving you. Your energy is a huge aspect of passion. The energy you have for what you do is a direct reflection of whether you believe in your own vision. Purpose and passion are linked.

When you feel connected with and walk in your purpose, you will always lead with more passion.

Consider: the questions I want you to ask yourself right now are...

Do I live with passion every day?
How do I attack the day?
How do I attack my goals, dreams, and aspirations?

Focus

Focus is how you spend every minute of your day. How you stack your day, your time, and your calendar against what you hope to achieve is the result of your focus.

This is where the lessons I shared from the chapter about "incremental not monumental" really hit home for my team and me. I'll go into more detail about focus and time management in a later chapter to refine this area if you need to do so.

Consider: How do I spend each minute of every day?

Take some time and do an audit on what gets your attention and whether this aligns with your values and goals.

Intentionality

When you master intentionality, you must consider: what do my words convey, and how can I be intentional in what I say? I often compare our process of growth to a building. Regardless of whether it's a one-story, a two-story, or a 30-story building, every story has its own floor with its own ceiling. The same is true for us. Whatever level you're on now there is a ceiling you must rise above. As we grow and level up, we continually identify the next ceiling or hurdle.

The temptation for us can be to take the elevator (a shortcut) when we see the multiple stories ahead of us, but we need to take the stairs. We need those incremental steps and not focus on monumental tasks. We must be intentional with our actions on the current level to rise to the next.

Intentionality requires us to build and use the muscles we have now while improving ourselves. I can attest that taking the right actions and preparing will open the next level up to you faster than you ever dreamed possible. I see it in my life and in the Grow Stack Drive community members as well.

Intentionality is so important as a filter because it has a profound effect on your passion. If you want to figure out your truest passion, start with your intention. Your intention will fuel your passion and your passion will drive your focus. These all work in harmony so you can level up.

Consider: What is the ceiling of the floor I am on right now?

What incremental actions should I be intentional about right now to get me to level up?
What does it look like when I arrive at the next level in my life?
What obstacle will I face at the next level?
Which skills prepare me to face that obstacle?

TEACHABILITY

At Grow Stack Drive, we define teachability as open to and *actively searching* for feedback. You must consider if you are engaging in a feedback loop. If you are not teachable, I do not want to be around you. Have a teachable heart. None of us knows everything. You and I must be coachable to advance our lives and our business. We have to speak into the issues we face.

Teachability comprises a couple of different factors. The first of which is asking brilliant questions. Great leaders ask great questions. The second aspect is when you get around outstanding leaders, don't be in a hurry to talk. I had to learn to listen for this to work in my life. When you get into an environment with prominent minds, be quiet and become like a sponge.

If you want to have a teachable spirit, frankly, just shut up. If you want to be teachable, or lead the next generation, learn to get neutral, get emotions in check, and take a moment to think. In being teachable, you also achieve great clarity.

Another great way to learn from mentors you may not have in-person access to is through books. A few books that have affected my life have been: *Three Feet from Gold* by Dr. Greg Reid, *21 Irrefutable Laws of Leadership* by Dr. John Maxwell, *Leaders Eat Last* by Simon Sinek, *The Advantage* by Patrick Lencioni, and *The Obstacle is the Way* by Ryan Holiday.

Consider: What resources and what people do I currently have available to me? What room can I get in and listen more than I speak?

FLEXIBILITY

Flexibility is the consideration of fluidity. When I think of flexibility, I think of the fact that I am fluid because the world is fluid. Flexibility is being open to change and being able to adjust as needed or when concerns arise. If you aren't willing to bend, you will break. Being flexible is about removing the idea that you have to be set in your ways. Don't settle into your comfort zone or be the person who will not change his or her mind.

A glaring example of flexibility would be the recent COVID-19 outbreak. Businesses that were flexible and fluid not only survived but thrived. Most businesses that weren't flexible have shut their doors.

Flexibility is one of the Grow Stack Drive filters because you have to be flexible to achieve any level of success. We are required to have flexibility as parents (if you are one), leaders, and humans. The world is going to throw you curveballs—some you will never expect! With flexibility you can adjust and move forward more prosperously from those situations.

Consider: What ways can I be more flexible?

TAKE ACTION NOW:

If you ran all the decisions you made today through these filters, would you make the same ones? Why or why not?

11
WINNING EVERY DAY

Time is the most finite resource we have available. We all have the same time available to us. Yet some of us are achieving more than others. It comes down to how you spend each of your 24 hours (remember: INCREMENTAL). The single most critical factor that weighs on your success is how you spend every hour.

The calendar is one of the best tools for establishing and reaching your goals. I have used many calendar formats and styles over the last few years to accelerate my business and take charge of my day. Time blocking is a simple thing you can do to establish a proper strategy for success with your time.

I'll share with you exactly how I do it and you are welcome to use this same technique. You can use the same method I do in any store-bought planner, or you can purchase one I made for the Grow Stack

Drive community. Just visit GrowStackDrive.com to learn more.

It's important to note,
the real secret to my winning every
day starts with the night before.

Before I go to bed, I fill out my calendar for the next day. I know what I'm going to do tomorrow before I close my eyes and rest.

Why is this so important? I've found if you spend the time before you go to bed at night looking at the calendar, you're excited about what's happened on this day and more capable of showing gratitude for it. You're not waking up in the morning and being reactive to the day because you know exactly what's going to happen.

As I look at my calendar, the first rule I use is stacking my time using four color-coded categories. These are the basis of how I spend my time. This is how I code my calendar:

BLUE: personal development
GREEN: where I make my money
YELLOW: where I work on the business
RED: family time

I make sure those are all on my calendar because they dictate how I intentionally spend my day.

The first is blue, and this is my personal time. When I wake up, I like to have quiet time. I will read scripture or expand my mind by reading a chapter of a personal development book, listen to a podcast, or complete a training. When I finish my quiet time in the morning, I'll open the Grow Stack Drive planner and write my goals down. My last activity for blue is fitness. Every morning my alarm goes off at 4:30 a.m. and I am in the gym by 5:30 a.m. Blue time is nonnegotiable for me.

Then I use green for time management. This time is for making money. If you don't have them yet, you need to set green blocks up on your calendar. Block out the time with green that you dedicate to making money.

The third block is yellow. For me, this is where I work **on** my business, not in my business. The yellow blocks are where I have conversations with future clients or follow through on various mentors and coaching opportunities I get. This is the time I spend building my brand. Even if it doesn't translate into immediate revenue, it's a must. So whether I'm calling clients, having lunch with a client, or sending out thank you cards, I'm intentional and adding value by working on my business and planning. I hope that gives you a good idea how to use those yellow blocks of time.

The last block is red, and this time is the most important to me. That's my heart. Red is all about family time. Make certain you put red blocks on your calendar. You must include family time and personal time on your calendar. For me, I block out time I spend with my daughters. That time is literally on my calendar as father-daughter time. Whether we're on the road to go get tacos at the local taco truck or whatever adventure we plan, I carve that time onto my calendar. Some people may think that's crazy, but relationships with those who matter don't happen unless we are intentional about the time we invest in them.

When you are defining your measurement for any time strategy, follow the Grow Stack Drive Code time blocking categories. Include these blocks of time in your daily and weekly actions. Use each of these to not only plan, but also assess how you are using your time. Make adjustments often and intentionally.

I created the Grow Stack Drive planner to hit on every aspect of winning and help my clients. Visit GrowStackDrive.com to purchase my customized planner that comes with easy-to-use format where you can write the key items you plan to focus on for that day and color code them. You will also find two places, one in the morning and one in the evening, to write your goals out. We also believe in writing out daily what you are grateful for, the top three things you are working on, what your wins are, and how you can be 1% better than the day before.

You'll also find a scoreboard printed for every day. Picture a t-ball game. There are tons of energetic adults, excitement from the stands, and kids screaming and running everywhere. Some are picking their nose and chasing butterflies in the outfield. If you look in the stands their families are going nuts. Grandma, grandpa, aunts, uncles, brothers, sisters, everybody is screaming as little Johnny hits the ball off the tee. He runs to third base, and the coach has to catch him and then point him in the right direction to home plate. It's lively and bustling. The problem is when you leave the game, nobody knows who won because you don't keep score. So, I also put a scoreboard in the planner to do just that.

We live in the real world where you have to keep score to know if you win.

Don't take my word for how transformative a schedule can be. My client Charlie messaged me and said by becoming intentional with his schedule, he's made huge financial gains. His normal February sales were at \$30k. This past February, he made \$203k in sales. He said the planner helped him break through the barriers to realizing his potential.

AFFIRMATION:

Every positive action I take accelerates my progress.

TAKE ACTION NOW:

How do you spend your time? Are you strategic in your blocking? Identify the four actions you need to take to propel your life and business forward.

Special note to the leader:

If you have reached this far in the book and want tactical, hands-on, personalized advice, reach out to me. Whether you're stuck or experiencing exponential growth, our proven methodology provides leaders and entrepreneurs with scalable and sustainable strategies to grow your business. Executives dive deep with our A4 process: Assessment --> Attention --> Action --> Accountability. We provide the framework you need, paired with a plan, to ensure you have the confidence, clarity, and community needed to set and crush Big Hairy Audacious Goals. Visit GrowStackDrive.com to learn more about A4.

SECTION 3

CREATE COMMUNITY

This section is all about how one can multiply your impact, leadership, and team to achieve more. There is more to being an outstanding leader than simply being successful. You'll get a unique spin on how you can achieve more success by not focusing on it at all. This section will take you on a journey of self-exploration, leadership development, and the creation of your own individual legacy.

12
SIGNIFICANCE VS. SUCCESS

People always ask me what it means to be successful. I want you to unwrap your current thinking about success, and consider something far bigger: ***significance***.

When I was a youth pastor in my early thirties, I spoke all over the United States at conferences. One of my first major opportunities was in April 2000 in Michigan with my mentor, Ron Luce. I was featured in the lineup between John Maxwell and another mentor, Jeanne. Jeanne was my spiritual mentor/spiritual mom and ran one of the largest youth ministries in America. It honored me to share that day with these successful thought leaders and speak in front of thousands of people.

The next day, Jeanne took me to lunch, sat me down, and with an intense look she said: "Ken, I want to ask you a very important question. Do you want to be significant, or do you want to be successful?" I was smart enough to answer it correctly, but I didn't *really* know what she was talking about. Jeanne said that if you live a life of significance, your mission becomes helping the people *around you* win and achieve.

If you start your work
with the goal of significance,
you'll always find success.

If you begin with the goal of simply finding success, you may or may not be significant. And you'll probably leave a trail of damage along the way.

As a 32-year-old on stage among my mentors, I thought I had arrived. Jeanne recognized it was the right time in my career to have this conversation with me, and I'm so grateful that she did. This was my first kind of big speaking event, which was huge for me, but Jeanne knew the trap and the allure of being in those kinds of positions. When we talk about significance versus success, that is where I learned that lesson and really is the foundation of everything that I do.

There is a two-fold process to this. First, seek significance. If you help those around you find success, you will always be successful. Second, get in rooms with people who think bigger than you do. I always find the key to growth is in relationships.

There are three spheres of relationships we all need. First is our *community*. This is the larger group of people we connect with. People that have similar passions & dreams as we do. The second is our *circle*. These are the 10-12 people that we spend time with regularly. The third is smaller and it's our *corner*. These are the 1-2 people that know everything about us and what's going on in our life.

If you get that relationship component right, it will help your mindset because you're around people who challenge you. Community gives us encouragement, and it brings us accountability. In a healthy and thriving community, accountability feels like encouragement, which is what I have inside the Grow Stack Drive private Facebook group.

I want to take the time to differentiate between significant leaders and successful leaders. See if you can find yourself in these descriptions.

Significant Leaders

Significant leaders focus on creating massive results and reproducing themselves through impact. Significance is about not only how much you achieve or the monetary gain but your return on mission. Leaders who strive to be significant are those who are more focused on multiplying and leading other leaders than on the personal gains that come from being called a leader.

SUCCESSFUL LEADERS

Successful leaders focus on the next advancement or the next story to tell. Success is personal. It is what someone seeks when they want gains for themselves. Leaders who seek success are ones that largely focus on the return on investment, accolades, and recognition they receive when they become or continue to be successful. Typically, being successful does not include taking care of others or building one another up. Success-focused leaders are inherently selfish. Since success is deeply personal, each team member may have a different idea of what success is, which could lead to confusion.

The most important thing to remember in being successful versus leading with significance is this: significance will always bring success. Success does not always ensure significance.

"If I pursue success, my joy is the result of my success; if I pursue significance, my joy is the result of others' success." —John Maxwell

AFFIRMATION:

I choose significance over success every day.

ACTION:

Do you want to be significant or successful? Why? Next, list five leaders you believe are living a life of significance and write down what they all have in common.

13
MULTIPLICATION

One of the most deeply personal and important aspects of being an effective leader is the ability to multiply oneself. This chapter helps individuals and business executives to ensure that they leave their legacy, significance, and growth to a team or company that continuously performs without them having to be in the thick of things.

I believe leadership is the ability to focus one's energy on the success of others. My goal is that by the end of this book, I can help maximize your leadership potential by no longer leading yourself, but by leading others most effectively. You'll feel empowered and encouraged to multiply through this process.

Throughout this chapter, I will challenge you to think critically and test yourself as a leader. This makes you think outside of what you have always known, take massive action, and show up as an authentic and multiplication-focused leader.

I am honored to lead you through one of the most powerful tools I have ever used. I first learned this rule of multiplication when our youth ministry exploded in growth over 18 months. We grew from just a handful of students to a few hundred students in that time period. How did we do that? By building and developing leaders. That is the power of multiplication.

My sincere desire for you is to maximize your potential by reframing what leadership means to you, causing a chain reaction within your organization. I want to clarify any misconceptions you may have about multiplication: what it is and what it is not. This will help eliminate confusion as you move forward and set up effective multiplication for yourself personally and professionally.

Multiplication is about leading leaders, growing your business, and affecting authentically. It is about creating an environment where people can thrive. Multiplication is about building up your business with committed people.

Multiplication is to increase growth beyond what is typically done at any given time. Furthermore, it is to increase by way of leading *other* leaders to their growth in both income and mission. Leaders who can multiple can create and leave legacies. They are able to create more opportunities for future leaders while leaving an impact of significance on the world around them.

Leaders who multiply are passionate leaders. They are leaders who are intentional about adding value to other's lives and anyone they lead. They are intentional about adding value to the company they keep around them. They are intentional about leaving a legacy far beyond what they thought was possible. They do all of this authentically.

Multiplication is not about how much money you make. In fact, money doesn't define or guarantee your ability to multiply your impact. If you focus entirely on money, you will only get a fraction of what you can achieve.

Great leaders are not concerned with how much money they make, accolades they collect, or how much they own. They are always focused on how many other people they take along the journey with them. These leaders see every team member as an asset and work tirelessly to encourage and grow.

The best way to reach your full leadership capacity is to run your leadership through the Grow Stack Drive filters. Answer the below questions about where you are right now as a leader before moving on to the next section.

PASSION:

What are you most passionate about?

Do you have a passion for what you do and are doing as a leader? Why or why not?

FOCUS:

How are you currently spending your time?

Are you finding it easy to stay on task?

Do you accomplish what you set out to do every day?

How are you focusing your time and energy on the goals at hand and achieving them?

TEACHABILITY:

Do you seek feedback? If so, how often?

Are you comfortable seeking and receiving feedback?

Are you actively seeking and accepting feedback?

Do you openly give feedback? Why or why not?

INTENTIONALITY:

Do you work with intentionality?

Are you intentional in your current communications?

If not, how can you make improvements?

FLEXIBILITY:

How do you react when things do not go as planned or you don't reach your goal?

How can you continuously show flexibility in your current role and for those who you lead?

AFFIRMATION

I am 100% committed to living a life of significance.

ACTION

Revisit the list of the five leaders you made at the end of the last chapter. How has each one used the Grow Stack Drive Code filters to lead with significance?

14

BUILDING A SIGNIFICANT TEAM

A lot of leaders and wannabe leaders shy away from a conversation or confrontation because they don't want to hurt someone when, in actuality, we do more damage by not confronting the situation. I want you to understand that it's actually *less* caring to stay silent.

When building a team and multiplying, you need to have conversations of all kinds. You cannot steer away from a conversation that needs to happen because you are uncomfortable.

Most people would rather avoid conflict at all costs than handle a situation head-on and move on. If you can't effectively manage conflict, you cannot multiply. The first step to handling conflict well is to understand what causes conflict to begin with.

The biggest cause of conflict is unclear expectations.

Expectations are key in handling conflicts. If someone is unclear what the expectations are of them or their work, there will always be conflict. Confusion leads to conflict, always. Setting clear expectations from the beginning of any project or working relationship and adjusting as often as necessary will keep expectations clear and objectives achievable.

The second largest cause for conflict is differing beliefs.

When we approach conflict from our differences on a deep level, we bring in our own personal grievances and issues. The difference in beliefs can create more tension than any other aspect. We must be teachable, flexible, and willing to see another perspective when approaching conflict. For when we do not—when we are too steadfast in our own beliefs—conflict arises.

Once you master the art of handling conflict, you can easily grow a team of significance. Here are a few of the best strategies I implement in my business and coach others to do the same.

Create Heros

Your team's success is a direct reflection of you as a leader. Adversely, your success as a leader is a direct reflection of their success as an employee. Leaders who spend more time creating heroes out of those they lead rather than focusing on their own personal successes will always achieve more. Not only that, but they are more likely to lead *more leaders* further. Remember, significant leaders lift those around them. Successful leaders use others to lift themselves.

Bring People In

Collaboration is key to great leadership, especially regarding goal setting and actions that will deeply affect the team. Bring people in on planning sessions, goal setting, and new ideas for the business. When people feel heard they trust more. They work harder. And, they are more likely to succeed.

Personalize and Invest in Development Plans—for Everyone.

Everyone has a different idea of success. Focus on developing every team member you have. Be fully invested in their personal and career development. Encourage them to seek opportunities that align with their goals for themselves, not just you or the company.

Celebrate. Celebrate. Celebrate.

Celebrate wins on all scales. Get to know what your team needs in terms of encouragement, what they resonate with, how they like to be celebrated. Then *do it.* Celebrating doesn't have to be elaborate, but it does need to be consistent. To get your team in the habit of celebrating their wins, you may consider using the Grow Stack Drive planner. It contains a space to write down wins daily. Teach your people to look for wins and watch how fast you build a team based on significance.

To have a healthy team, everyone must understand what game they should be playing. The patterns of the game aren't decided by the rules of the game but by the number of people participating. Some people that you are close to won't want to make the shift when it's time. What will you do to encourage them? What do you need to do to step up as a leader for everyone, even if they are not 100% on board?

AFFIRMATION:

I help people to be the best they can be.

ACTION:

How do you see yourself as a leader based on the four stages discussed above? Where is an area you can take incremental action today?

15
DEVELOP OTHERS

Life is very much like driving in a car. We stare out the windshield to see where to go, but we also have a rearview mirror. That rearview mirror is the past. If you live life always looking in the rearview mirror, you will crash!

LEARN from the past, don't LIVE in it!

In the same regard, every one of us has blind spots. That's why we need a community of people around us who are going after the same things we are. I've taken great care to build a community of like-minded entrepreneurs who all want to achieve significance. I describe the Grow Stack Drive community like this: if the church I planted and 10X had a baby, that's the Grow Stack Drive community.

Remember the earlier discussion on teachability? Are you actively pursuing feedback? I want to test your current community and have you conduct an experiment this week. I want you to find one person and ask, "Hey, what am I missing?" See how honestly and transparently they answer. How often do you have those kinds of conversations with someone? Do you have an entire community of people that will have hard conversations? I do within my circle because it's the only way for me to continually improve.

Grant Cardone often quotes Proverbs 27:17: "As iron sharpens iron, so one person sharpens another." So be around people going in the same direction as you and who will lift you up. You need to be around people who are encouraging you. I saw a quote on Instagram that really outlined this best. It said, "If your circle of friends aren't helping you get better, it's not a circle; it's a cage."

Your greatest asset is not necessarily the money in your bank account; it's the people you've surrounded yourself with. They're the ones that alert us to our blind spots and call the best out of us. They are there to guide us and give wisdom. I know that's what the Grow Stack Drive family is all about; it's creating a circle that can call into the depths of one another.

Thermometers and Thermostats

I want to close by sharing the most fundamental way to develop others. It starts by recognizing there are two types of people. A thermometer is somebody who just gauges the temperature of the room. A thermostat is a person who walks in the room and can change the culture and the temperature of a room—any room they walk into. So here's the question I want you to ask yourself: when you walk into a room, do people gravitate away from you or toward you? Because here's the deal, you want to find success, or you wouldn't be reading this book. You want to turn the incremental into monumental and be the type of person people gravitate toward when you walk in a room.

You must act with intentionality to be someone who can set the temperature of what you're trying to accomplish. When you're a thermostat, you raise the level of energy wherever you go. People gravitate toward energy and passion. When you are intentional, you can create change. If you're a thermostat, you're an agent of change. That means wherever you go, whatever you do, you're creating change, and you're helping others. You're serving without being asked.

We all know these people. My friend Nate May nailed this on a recent live video in our community. He said, "I'm not talking about your personality. I'm not talking about introverts and extroverts. I'm not talking about walking into a room and yelling or being loud. I'm talking about walking into a room and being intentional about your surroundings." When you engage in the conversation, do you ask quality questions? Are you the one just standing by, hoping maybe someone else will start the conversation? Or are you sitting there asking questions that lead to the depths of somebody?

People know when they see authenticity in someone, and they can sniff out a fake really quick. So be someone who actually sets the temperature and the mood in a room. Those are the game-changers. Thermostats have a magical way of always making it about the other person. It's never about them.

Who do you want to hang out with, a thermometer or a thermostat? I've asked people who wanted to be a pastor or who wanted to start a business which one they were. You could literally see someone's mood sink when they know the answer is a thermometer. So if that is you, don't be discouraged. You can change, and I can tell you how you can do it.

I want you to become an encourager. Passionate leaders are intentional about adding value. I'm constantly making contact within my community. I'm not asking for anything. I'm just adding value. Even if it's simply wishing a happy birthday to my Facebook friends. Crush your limiting beliefs of insecurity by being *interested*, not interesting.

When you walk into a room, are you interested in the other people in it, or do you want people interested in you? When you are authentic and really have a desire to know what's going on with another person during a conversation, you'll change from being a thermometer to a thermostat.

I've seen this concept transform people from a thermometer to a thermostat. There are members of the Grow Stack Drive community who I've watched take this advice and become intentional in their care for others. Now those folks are sought after by the leadership in their company. The beauty of being a thermostat is you don't just attract the attention of your peers. You draw the attention of those who you want to serve. The ones you want to run with in life. If you're looking to advance your life and your career personally, professionally, or financially, become a thermostat.

And finally, if you want to be a thermostat, you better become a person who asks great questions and listens to the answers. We are living in a time where there's more content produced every day than ever before in history. There are so freaking many people talking! Everyone is talking and just not listening. The problem is that these content producers rarely have anything of value to say.

I tell you all of this because I have some big, hairy audacious goals. And I don't hide them! It's no secret I want to speak to bigger audiences and get more clients. But, you know how I'm going to reach those goals? I'm going to do it by being a thermostat. I'm going to do it by adding value. I'm building relationships with people in such a way that it makes a difference in their personal life and in their businesses.

If you take only one thing from this book, let it be this: walk slowly through the crowd and pay attention to people. Be present when someone speaks. Listen—*actively listen*—when you are in a conversation.

If you're ready to get into a room with people who are thermostats and who will level you up, consider joining the Grow Stack Drive community at GrowStackDrive.com.

ABOUT THE AUTHOR

CEO of the Ken Joslin Team & the GROW STACK DRIVE brand, Ken is a 10X Master Coach, Grant Cardone Licensee, and real estate professional. Ken Joslin is a driven leader who has closed over $250mm in real estate transactions. He has planted multiple churches, and mentored hundreds. He is passionate about helping business leaders Build Confidence, Gain Clarity & Create Community. More than that, Ken is a generous father, and friend.

Made in the USA
Monee, IL
07 November 2021